People Who Help

Firefighters

by Nancy Dickmann

raintree

a Capstone company — publishers for children

Raintree is an imprint of Capstone Global Library Limited, a company incorporated in England and Wales having its registered office at 264 Banbury Road, Oxford, OX2 7DY – Registered company number 6695582

www.raintree.co.uk
myorders@raintree.co.uk

Produced by Brown Bear Books Ltd:
Text: Nancy Dickmann
Design Manager: Keith Davis
Editorial Director: Lindsey Lowe
Children's Publisher: Anne O'Daly
Picture Manager: Sophie Mortimer
Printed and bound in India

ISBN: 978-1-4747-5548-1 (hardback)
21 20 19 18 17
10 9 8 7 6 5 3 2 1

ISBN: 978-1-4747-5552-8 (paperback)
22 21 20 19 18
10 9 8 7 6 5 3 2 1

British Library Cataloguing-in-Publication Data
A full catalogue record for this book is available from the British Library.

Acknowledgements
We would like to thank the following for permission to reproduce photographs:
Alamy: Dorset Media Service, 5 (top), Eye Candy Images, 4, Adrian Sherratt, 7, Jack Sullivan, 15; Dreamstime: Martin Brayley, 12, Monkey Business Images, 1; iStock: Birzio, 13, kelvinjay, 6, wcjohnston, 10; Kent Fire & Emergency Service: 8, 9, 14, 17, 18, 19, 20, 21; Shutterstock: Gary Perkin, 15, Monkey Business Images, cover; ukemergency: Richard Thompson, 11; UKNIP: Jason Kay, 5 (bottom right)

Brown Bear Books has made every attempt to contact copyright holders of material reproduced in this book. Any omissions will be rectified in subsequent printings if notice is given to the publisher. If anyone has any information please contact licensing@brownbearbooks.co.uk

Contents

Some words are shown in bold, **like this**. You can find out what they mean by looking in the glossary.

Here comes a fire engine!

A fire engine speeds down the road.
It is in a hurry. Its **sirens** and flashing lights
warn cars to get out of the way.

Firefighters help people in an **emergency**. They put out fires. They help at accidents and disasters. Firefighters rescue people from all types of situation.

What firefighters do

A fire can start at any time, day or night. Firefighters must always be ready to help. Fast response saves lives.

First aid

Firefighters are often the first people to arrive at the scene of an **emergency**. They rescue people who need help. Firefighters are trained in **first aid**.

The control room

An **emergency** call comes into the **control room**. The **dispatcher** asks the caller questions about the fire.

The dispatcher notes down the details. He or she decides how many fire engines to send. The firefighters are ready and waiting. They race to the fire engine.

Firefighting vehicles

Firefighters travel in a fire engine. It has hoses for pumping water. Cupboards on the sides hold the firefighters' **equipment**.

Storage cupboards

Fire and rescue boat

Firefighters use boats for **emergencies** on rivers. They rescue people from ships that are sinking or on fire. The boats have pumps that use river water to put out fires.

Fighting a fire

The firefighters quickly study the fire. They see if anyone needs to be rescued. Then they decide who will do each job.

Planning

Firefighters have long ladders. Some fire engines have cradles to lift firefighters higher into the air. They use hoses to spray strong jets of water on a fire.

Special tools

Breathing smoke is dangerous. Firefighters wear special masks. The masks are connected to **oxygen** tanks. Firefighters wear the tanks on their backs.

Air tank

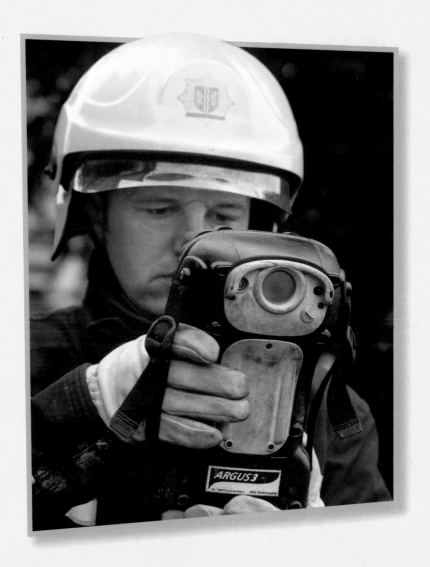

Firefighters use special cameras that show body heat. They show the firefighters where people are trapped.

Helping at accidents

Firefighters also help other **emergency** services at road accidents. They rescue people trapped in cars. Sometimes they have to cut the car apart.

If dangerous **chemicals** are spilled, firefighters can help. They wear special **protective clothing**. They make sure the chemicals do not spread.

Keeping busy

Firefighters keep busy as they wait for the next call. They check their **equipment** to make sure it is ready when they are needed.

Members of the fire and rescue service visit factories, offices and shops. They check that fire safety rules are being followed. They check fire exits and **fire extinguishers**.

Teaching the public

Firefighters often visit schools. They talk to children about their job. They show them the fire engine and explain how they fight fires.

Smoke alarm

Firefighters also visit people in their homes. These visits are called Safe and Well visits. Firefighters check plug sockets and electrical wiring. They install and test **smoke alarms**.

Staying safe

Always remember:

🪜 Never play with fire or matches.

🪜 Ask your parents to test the smoke alarm regularly.

🪜 Call 999 in an emergency.

🪜 Make sure you know your address. You will need to tell the dispatcher your address if you call 999.

Glossary

chemical a substance used in or produced by a chemical process. Some chemicals are dangerous

control room room where dispatchers answer emergency calls and send out fire crews

dispatcher person who answers calls and decides what type of help to send

emergency serious situation, such as a fire or road accident, that calls for fast action

equipment items that a person needs to do their job

fire extinguisher something that puts a fire out

first aid emergency medical help given while waiting for a doctor

oxygen gas in the air that people need to breathe

protective clothing clothing that protects the body

siren warning device that makes a loud noise

smoke alarm object that makes a loud noise if it senses smoke

Find out more

Books

Firefighter (Here to Help), Rachel Blount (Franklin Watts, 2017)

Firefighter (People Who Help Us), Rebecca Hunter (Tulip Books, 2014)

Firefighters to the Rescue Around the World (To the Rescue!), Linda Staniford (Raintree, 2017)

Ten Fire Engines and Emergency Vehicles (Cool Machines), Chris Oxlade (Franklin Watts, 2017)

Websites

www.cambsfire.gov.uk/about-us/fleet-and-equipment.aspx
Learn about fire engines and firefighting equipment

www.hantsfire.gov.uk/kidzone-and-schools/play-games/
Try out games and activities about firefighting

Index